THE
SPIRIT-FILLED
LIFE

THE SPIRIT-FILLED LIFE

What It Means To Walk in Love,
in Light, and in Wisdom

Dr. R. Timothy Jones

FORWARD PRESS
SHREVEPORT, LOUISIANA

Copyright © Dr. R. Timothy Jones (Forward Press)

Unless otherwise indicated, all Scripture references are taken from the New King James Version. Copyright © 1979, 1980, 1982 by Thomas Nelson, Inc. Used by permission. All rights reserved.

Scripture quotations marked ESV® are taken from the Bible (The Holy Bible, English Standard Version®), copyright © 2001 by Crossway, a publishing ministry of Good News Publishers. Used by permission. All rights reserved.

Scripture quotations marked MSG are taken from *The Message*, copyright © 1993, 2002, 2018 by Eugene H. Peterson. Used by permission of NavPress. All rights reserved. Represented by Tyndale House Publishers.

Scripture quotations marked NLT are taken from the *Holy Bible*, New Living Translation, Copyright © 1996, 2004, 2015 by Tyndale-House Foundation. Used by permission of Tyndale House Publishers, Inc., Carol Stream, Illinois 60188. All rights reserved.

Scripture quotations marked NIV are taken from the Holy Bible, New International Version®, NIV®. Copyright © 1973, 1978, 1984, 2011 by Biblica, Inc.™ Used by permission of Zondervan. All rights reserved worldwide. www.zondervan.com. The "NIV" and "New International Version" are trademarks registered in the United States Patent and Trademark Office by Biblica, Inc.™

Be filled with the Spirit.
EPHESIANS 5:18

CONTENTS

I. INTRODUCTION 9

II. LESSONS 13

    1. Meet the Holy Spirit 13

    2. Three Types of People 31

    3. What Is the Spirit-Filled Life? 47

    4. Be Imitators of God 65

    5. Matters of Morality 83

    6. Children of the Light 101

    7. Fruitless Deeds of Darkness 121

    8. Walk Circumspectly 139

III. EPILOGUE — Marks of Maturity 157

INTRODUCTION

*Breathe in me, O Holy Spirit,
that my thoughts may all be holy.*

*Act in me, O Holy Spirit,
that my work, too, may be holy.*

*Draw my heart, O Holy Spirit,
that I love but what is holy.*

*Strengthen me, O Holy Spirit,
to defend all that is holy.*

*Guard me, then, O Holy Spirit,
that I always may be holy. Amen.*

Saint Augustine

Jesus promised that believers would never be alone or without comfort. The Holy Spirit represents the abiding presence of God in our lives. Without such, we would be like orphans, without the love and support of caring parents (John 14:18).

There are many erroneous beliefs when it comes to the Holy Spirit. The third member of the Godhead has even been treated like an afterthought in the Trinity. Some relegate the Holy Spirit to emotional responses in worship. However, the Holy Spirit is our Comforter, Teacher, and Guide.

Ephesus was a major political, commercial, and religious center in Asia Minor (modern-day Turkey). Though the region was heavily pagan, the church flourished during Paul's three-year evangelistic tenure there. However, Revelation 2:4 conveys that somewhere along the way, they left their first love.

Ephesians was written from a Roman prison around 60 CE by Paul, who referred to himself as an "ambassador in chains" (6:20). Unlike Paul's other writings, this letter does not address any particular problem. It might have even been a circular letter to churches in the area. Ephesians identifies who we are in Christ: "We are God's masterpiece" (2:10 NLT). It always emphasizes Christian living.

This book is based on Ephesians 5, in which Paul perfectly weds faith and practice. Paul accentuates the Spirit-filled life by illustrating what it means to walk in love (v. 2), in light (v. 8), and in wisdom (v. 15).

The Spirit-Filled Life was written as a resource for discipleship. It was designed to be a journey, not just a study. It integrates didactic and devotional approaches to studying the Holy Spirit. There are lessons to help readers understand and appreciate the Spirit, as well as devotional work to help readers personally experience the Holy Spirit daily.

While this book can be read individually, it is best used in small-group settings over several weeks. There is an African proverb that says, "If you want to go fast, go alone. If you want to go far, go together."

God designed the body of Christ with a sense of interdependence. Ecclesiastes 4:9 says, "Two are better than one." Thus, we believe spiritual growth happens best in community. Small groups offer several benefits, such as accountability, connection, and encouragement. Each week we should grow stronger individually and collectively. We are truly better together.

The Spirit-Filled Life has several intended outcomes. The first intended outcome is to equip believers to "grow in the grace and the knowledge of the Lord Jesus Christ" (2 Peter 3:18). That is the objective of spiritual maturity.

Secondly, this book seeks to create a deeper awareness of the personality and the ministry of the Holy Spirit. Readers are also encouraged to live spiritually versus naturally or carnally. This entails being led by the Spirit rather than the flesh.

The lessons are both concise and precise with the goal of engaging the reader in enlightening and exciting ways. Daily passages were selected to complement the lesson for the week. Quotes and motivational sayings are provided for daily inspiration. Prayer prompts are provided to reflect on the reader's spiritual condition.

Students should spend about fifteen minutes each day studying the daily verses, pondering each day's voices, and claiming each day's victory. The daily work is not long but is designed to be impactful. We pray that our lives are never the same as a result of this journey with the Holy Spirit.

Let's grow!

—Dr. R. Timothy Jones

LESSON ONE

MEET THE HOLY SPIRIT

*"Without the Spirit of God, we can do nothing.
We are as ships without wind. We are useless."*

Charles Spurgeon

MEET THE HOLY SPIRIT

"The Holy Spirit's main ministry is not to give thrills but to create in us Christlike character."

J. I. Packer

The Holy Spirit has been both misunderstood and misrepresented. The Holy Spirit has even been relegated to a feeling or an emotional experience in worship. Thank God, the Holy Spirit is with us beyond Sunday mornings.

Some denominational groups have ignored the Holy Spirit while others have focused on the Holy Spirit almost exclusively. It has even been suggested that today's believer should tarry for the Holy Spirit after conversion. The truth is we received the Holy Spirit at the time of our conversion.

> *If you know Jesus Christ as your Lord and Savior, you already have the Holy Spirit living within you.*
> **—David Jeremiah**

> *For by one Spirit we were all baptized into one body—whether Jews or Greeks, whether slaves or free—and have all been made to drink into one Spirit.*
> **—1 Corinthians 12:13 NKJV**

THE PERSONALITY OF THE HOLY SPIRIT

God has revealed Himself in three persons: God the Father, God the Son (Jesus Christ), and God the Holy Spirit. Thus, the Godhead is also called the Trinity. Though one person, each member of the Godhead has a distinct role in our lives.

God the Father is our Creator. He created us in His image and likeness and for His pleasure. Acts 17:28 (NKJV) says, "For in Him we live and move and have our being."

God the Son is Jesus Christ, who is our Redeemer or Savior. Romans 5:8 (NKJV) says, "While we were still sinners, Christ died for us."

God the Holy Spirit is our Comforter, our Teacher, and our Guide. John 16:13 (NIV) says, "When the Spirit of truth comes, he will guide you into all the truth."

> *Every divine action begins from the Father, proceeds through the Son, and is completed in the Holy Spirit.* —**Saint Basil**

The Holy Spirit is not a force, a power, or an influence but a person with a will and emotions. Reflecting the attributes of God, the Holy Spirit is also eternal (Hebrews 9:14), omnipresent (Psalm 139:7–10), and intelligent (1 Corinthians 2:10–11).

The Holy Spirit is represented in Scripture by a number of symbols, including:

1. **Dove** — Symbolizes purity and peace (Luke 3:22)

2. **Fire** — Embodies the presence of the Lord (Acts 2:3)

3. **Wind** — Indicates unseen power (John 3:8)

4. **Water** — Denotes life and cleansing (John 7:37–39)

5. **Seal** — Signifies ownership (Ephesians 4:30)

6. **Oil** — Represents light, healing, and anointing for service (Isaiah 61:1)

THE MINISTRY OF THE HOLY SPIRIT

The Holy Spirit convicts humanity regarding sin, righteousness, and judgment. The Holy Spirit also guides the believer into all truth

(John 16:8–15). It is the Holy Spirit who makes the new birth possible (John 3:6, Titus 3:5).

The baptism of the Holy Spirit takes place at conversion. It is when the Spirit places the new believer in the Body of Christ. 1 Corinthians 12:13 (NKJV) says, "By one Spirit we were all baptized into one body."

On four occasions, the Bible presents the Holy Spirit as our Comforter. The Greek term employed is *paraclete*, which means one called alongside another to help or assist. As our Comforter, the Holy Spirit dwells within us (John 14:17), bears witness of Jesus Christ (John 15:26–27), and guides us into all truth (John 16:13).

The Holy Spirit also convicts the world of sin, righteousness, and judgment (John 16:8–11). The late prominent evangelist Billy Graham said, "It is the Holy Spirit's job to convict, God's job to judge, and my job to love."

According to Ephesians 1:13–14 the believer is also sealed with the Holy Spirit. To be sealed is to be marked or branded, which shows ownership, identification, and security. The seal is the deposit or the guarantee of God's promises.

The believer also has the indwelling of the Holy Spirit. 1 Corinthians 6:19 (NKJV) asks, "Do you not know that your body is the temple of the Holy Spirit who is in you?" However, there is a difference between the indwelling of the Holy Spirit and the filling of the Holy Spirit.

The indwelling of the Holy Spirit is like having the Spirit as a passenger in your car. Being filled with the Holy Spirit is like having the Spirit drive the car. To be filled with the Holy Spirit is to surrender to the control of the Holy Spirit. The evidence of being filled with (or controlled by) the Holy Spirit is not the gifts of the Spirit but the fruit of the Spirit.

> *But the fruit of the Spirit is love, joy, peace, longsuffering, kindness, goodness, faithfulness, gentleness, self-control. Against such there is no law.* —**Galatians 5:22–23** NKJV

The Holy Spirit empowers the believer to share the good news of Jesus Christ. Acts 1:8 (NIV) says, "But you will receive power when the Holy Spirit comes on you; and you will be my witnesses in Jerusalem, and in all Judea and Samaria, and to the ends of the earth."

At times, believers do not know what we should pray for or find it difficult to pray. In those moments, the Holy Spirit intercedes on our behalf:

> *Likewise the Spirit also helps in our weaknesses. For we do not know what we should pray for as we ought, but the Spirit Himself makes intercession for us with groanings which cannot be uttered.* —**Romans 8:26 NKJV**

> *Prayer is not what is done by us, but rather what is done by the Holy Spirit in us.* —**Henri Nouwen**

The Holy Spirit provides spiritual gifts to believers for the edification of the Body of Christ. The gifts of the Holy Spirit are supernatural abilities to serve. 1 Peter 4:10 (NKJV) says, "As each one has received a gift, minister it to one another, as good stewards of the manifold grace of God."

There are at least eighteen spiritual gifts, including such things as administration, discernment, evangelism, healing, helps, hospitality, serving, tongues, teaching, and wisdom.[1] Ultimately, the gifts of the Spirit are for the glorification of God (1 Peter 4:11).

> *O Holy Spirit, descend plentifully into my heart. Enlighten the dark corners of this neglected dwelling and scatter there Thy cheerful beams.* —**Saint Augustine**

---

1. See 1 Corinthians 12, Ephesians 4:7–16, Romans 12:3–8, and 1 Peter 4:10–11.

DISCUSSION QUESTIONS

1. Explain the Godhead and the distinct roles of its members.

2. How is the Holy Spirit a person versus a power or an influence?

3. What is the role of the Holy Spirit in salvation? Elaborate.

4. Define the baptism of the Holy Spirit.

5. Discuss the significance of the three symbols of the Holy Spirit on the cover of this book.

6. Elaborate on the Holy Spirit's role as our Comforter.

7. What is the difference between the indwelling of the Holy Spirit and the filling of the Holy Spirit?

8. What does it mean to be sealed with the Holy Spirit?

9. Discuss the role of the Holy Spirit in prayer.

10. What is the evidence of being filled with the Holy Spirit?

11. List at least six gifts of the Spirit.

12. Read 1 Peter 4:10–11. Discuss the nature of spiritual gifts.

THE SPIRIT-FILLED LIFE

PRAYER

Father, thank You for not leaving us alone and without comfort. You have provided the gift of the Holy Spirit to guide us into all truth. Your Spirit brings Your peace, Your power, and most of all, Your presence. Thank You for sealing us with and sanctifying us by Your Spirit. Help us to walk after the Spirit and not after the flesh. Help us to yield more of ourselves to Your Spirit daily, thus bearing the fruit of Your Spirit. In the Name of Jesus Christ, our Lord, AMEN.

WEEK ONE

MONDAY

Today's Verses
Hebrews 9:11–15

Today's Voice
The Holy Spirit is the bond by which Christ efficaciously unites us to himself. —John Calvin

Today's Victory
Pray that God would purify your conscience from sinful deeds so that you can worship the living God.

TUESDAY

Today's Verses
Psalm 139:7–10

Today's Voice
Let yourselves be led by the Holy Spirit, with freedom and, please, do not cage the Holy Spirit. —**Pope Francis**

Today's Victory
Thank God for the omnipresence of the Holy Spirit and ask for a heart to be led by the Holy Spirit.

WEDNESDAY

Today's Verses
1 Corinthians 2:10–16

Today's Voice
I don't want the world to define God for me. I want the Holy Spirit to reveal God to me. —A. W. Tozer

Today's Victory
Pray that the Holy Spirit would open your mind to receive spiritual things.

THURSDAY

Today's Verses
1 Corinthians 6:18–20

Today's Voice
Take care of your body as if you were going to live forever; and take care of your soul as if you were going to die tomorrow. —Saint Augustine

Today's Victory
Celebrate your body as the temple of the Holy Spirit. Ask God to guard your heart from lust so that you may honor God with your body.

FRIDAY

Today's Verse

Acts 1:8

Today's Voice

True biblical love is compassionately and righteously pursuing the well-being of another. — Tony Evans

Today's Victory

Pray for the salvation of a lost family member or friend and trust the Holy Spirit to give you the boldness to witness to that person.

LESSON TWO

THREE TYPES OF PEOPLE

*"O Holy Spirit, descend plentifully into my heart.
Enlighten the dark corners of this neglected dwelling
and scatter there Thy cheerful beams."*

Saint Augustine

THREE TYPES OF PEOPLE

When I consider Your heavens, the work of Your fingers, the moon and the stars, which You have ordained, what is man that You are mindful of him, And the son of man that You visit him? — **Psalm 8:3–4** NKJV

> "I love humanity.
> It's people I can't stand."
>
> LINUS VAN PELT
> *PEANUTS* BY CHARLES SCHULZ

In the grand scheme of things, humans are miniscule. However, we have value in God. We are fearfully and wonderfully made in the image and likeness of God. Acts 17:28 (NKJV) says, "For in Him we live and move and have our being."

The Bible presents three types of people: the natural person, the carnal person, and the spiritual person. Natural people live apart from God and are ignorant of the things of God. Carnal people have experienced salvation but do not lead godly lives. Spiritual people live intimately with God and reflect His character in their lives.

Those who know the way to God can find it in the dark.
—**Alexander McLaren**

THE NATURAL PERSON

Thanks to Adam, sin is the "birth defect" of humanity. Romans 5:12 (NKJV) says, "Through one man sin entered the world." Thus, every person has a sin nature, an innate predisposition to sin. It is the self-seeking proclivity to do whatever we want.

The natural person is indifferent to God and the things of God. This person is a child of God through creation but not in Christ (Galatians 3:26). This person may not believe in God, they have not received Jesus Christ as Savior and Lord, and they are neither indwelt nor filled with the Holy Spirit.

> *The person without the Spirit does not accept the things that come from the Spirit of God but considers them foolishness.* —**1 Corinthians 2:14** NIV

The lives of natural people are driven by at least one of the three strongholds in 1 John 2:15–17: the lust of the flesh, the lust of the eyes, and the pride of life. According to Ephesians 2:3, the natural person seeks to gratify the cravings of the flesh and follows its desires and thoughts.

Natural people cannot understand or appreciate the "deep things of God" because they do not have the Holy Spirit. They reject God and His Word and consider godly things to be foolish. The natural person is subject to the wrath of God.

> *He who believes in the Son has everlasting life; and he who does not believe the Son shall not see life, but the wrath of God abides on him.* —**John 3:36** NKJV

The Carnal Person

> *Dear brothers and sisters, when I was with you, I couldn't talk to you as I would to spiritual people. I had to talk as though you belonged to this world or as though you were infants in Christ. I had to feed you with milk, not with solid food, because you weren't ready for anything stronger. And you still aren't ready, for you are still controlled by your sinful nature. You are jealous of one another and quarrel with each other. Doesn't that prove you are controlled*

by your sinful nature? Aren't you living like people of the world? —**1 Corinthians 3:1–3 NLT**

Some theologians only consider two types of people: the natural person (unsaved) and the spiritual person (saved). They make no distinction between natural people and carnal people. One significant difference between carnal people and natural people is that carnal people choose darkness over the light. Natural people may not have ever been exposed to the light.

In 1 Corinthians 3:1, Paul refers to spiritually immature people as "babes in Christ." They had to be fed with milk because they could not receive solid food. They were yet controlled by the sinful nature, jealous, and quarrelsome.

They are not growing in the grace and knowledge of the Lord Jesus Christ (2 Peter 3:18). They have accepted Jesus Christ as Savior but have not surrendered their lives to the lordship of Christ. The issue is most likely not salvation but rather sanctification.

Salvation and sanctification have been likened unto saving a drowning victim. To do so requires two steps: You must get the individual out of the water, and then you must get the water out of the individual. Salvation is getting people out of sin. Sanctification is getting sin out of people.

Thus, the carnal person has experienced the new birth but lives according to his or her carnal or fleshly desires. Unfortunately, the carnal person yet walks according to the flesh and not the Spirit.

A man once tried to describe the internal war between his flesh and his spirit. He said there were two dogs fighting inside of him. When asked which dog was winning, he said, "The one I feed the most!"

Everyone is confronted with the three strongholds in 1 John 2:15–17—lust, greed, and pride. However, the carnal person may not have a desire to be delivered from them. Carnal people often enjoy their sin.

THE SPIRITUAL PERSON

The spiritual person is a born-again believer who yields control of his or her life to the Holy Spirit. For them, Jesus Christ is both Savior and Lord. They are saved, sanctified, and filled with the Holy Spirit.

When asked if D. L. Moody had a monopoly on the Holy Spirit, someone replied, "No, but the Holy Spirit has a monopoly on Mr. Moody."

The spiritual person demonstrates spiritual maturity by growing "in the grace and knowledge of the Lord Jesus Christ" (2 Peter 3:18). They are "doers of the Word, and not hearers only" (James 1:22).

The life of the spiritual person is characterized by the fruit of the Spirit: love, joy, peace, longsuffering, kindness, goodness, gentleness, and self-control (Galatians 5:22–23). The spiritual person has crucified the flesh and its passions.

There Is Hope

Natural people can be saved. Since God loves all humanity, salvation is available to everyone. At Calvary, Jesus Christ died to reconcile humanity to God. To receive salvation, the natural person should simply "confess with [his or her] mouth the Lord Jesus and believe in [his or her] heart that God has raised Him from the dead, [and he or she] will be saved" (Romans 10:9 NKJV).

Carnal people can be sanctified. In 2 Timothy 2:22 (NIV), Paul commands, "Flee the evil desires of youth and pursue righteousness, faith, love and peace, along with those who call on the Lord out of a pure heart."

> *Outside of the cross of Jesus Christ, there is no hope in this world. That cross and resurrection at the core of the Gospel is the only hope for humanity.* —**Ravi Zacharias**

> *My hope is built on nothing less*
> *than Jesus' blood and righteousness;*
> *I dare not trust the sweetest frame,*
> *but wholly lean on Jesus' name.*
>
> *On Christ, the solid Rock, I stand:*
> *all other ground is sinking sand;*
> *all other ground is sinking sand.*[2]

---

2. "My Hope Is Built on Nothing Less," Edward Mote (1834)

Discussion Questions

1. Explain the nature of each of the following types of people.

    The natural person

    The carnal person

    The spiritual person

2. What are the differences between the natural person and the carnal person?

3. Which of the three types of people best describes you?

4. Can the natural person be saved? If so, how?

5. Discuss the hope for the carnal person.

6. Read 2 Peter 3:18. What does it mean to grow in the grace and knowledge of Jesus Christ?

Prayer

Our Heavenly Father, thank You for fearfully and wonderfully creating us in Your image and likeness. Unfortunately, our lives have not always reflected Your character. Forgive us for every carnal deed, word, and thought. May Your Holy Spirit help us to grow in the grace and knowledge of the Lord Jesus Christ. Amen.

WEEK TWO

MONDAY

Today's Verses
John 3:1–8, 16 & 36

Today's Voice
All individuals have the same value, not to be determined by market price. They're made in the image and likeness of God. —Cornel West

Today's Victory
If you are a born-again believer, thank God for your salvation. If you are not, confess Jesus Christ is Lord and ask Him to come into your heart.

TUESDAY

Today's Verses
1 John 2:15–17

Today's Voice
How can you pull down strongholds of Satan if you don't even have the strength to turn off your TV?
—Leonard Ravenhill

Today's Victory
Whether it is pride, greed, or lust, ask God to break the strongholds in your life and trust the Holy Spirit to deliver and/or defend you.

WEDNESDAY

TODAY'S VERSES
1 Corinthians 3:1–3

TODAY'S VOICE
We have supposed that the way to help people be holy is to just tell them to 'stop sinning' when in fact, lasting transformation is a spiritual consequence of beholding the glory of the Lord. —Jackie Hill Perry

TODAY'S VICTORY
Ask God to give you a greater hunger and thirst for righteousness.

THURSDAY

TODAY'S VERSES
Galatians 5:22–26

TODAY'S VOICE
You are who you are when no one is watching. —E. K. Bailey

TODAY'S VICTORY
Pray that the Holy Spirit would produce more fruit in your life and guard your heart from conceit and envy.

FRIDAY

TODAY'S VERSE

2 Timothy 2:22

TODAY'S VOICE

In order to discover the character of people we have only to observe what they love. — **Saint Augustine**

TODAY'S VICTORY

Pray that the Holy Spirit would lead you away from youthful lusts and guide you in the pursuit of righteousness, faith, love, and peace.

LESSON THREE

WHAT IS THE SPIRIT-FILLED LIFE?

"The Spirit-filled life is not a special, deluxe edition of Christianity. It is part and parcel of the total plan of God for His people."

A. W. TOZER

WHAT IS THE SPIRIT-FILLED LIFE?

And do not be drunk with wine, in which is dissipation; but be filled with the Spirit.

EPHESIANS 5:18 NKJV

"The same way that the Holy Spirit is to guide how you pray, let Him guide how you live."

JACKIE HILL PERRY

Once upon a time, a little boy was flying a kite. As the wind got stronger, the kite rose higher and higher until it was out of sight. A man passing by saw the boy but not the kite and asked, "How do you know there is a kite up there?" The boy replied, "Because I can feel it."

Such is the case with the Holy Spirit. Though we cannot see the Holy Spirit, we should feel the Spirit working in our lives.

Each of the three co-equal members of the Godhead has a unique role in our lives. God the Father created us in His image and for His pleasure. In Jesus Christ, we have been redeemed and forgiven "according to the riches of His grace" (Ephesians 1:7). The Holy Spirit guides us into all truth (John 16:13).

In the previous lesson, we explored three types of people found in the Bible. The natural person has not received Jesus Christ and cannot comprehend spiritual things. The carnal person has accepted Jesus Christ as Savior but lives in the natural state and walks according to the flesh. The spiritual person not only has experienced the new birth, but also has surrendered to the lordship of Jesus Christ. It is the spiritual person who is filled with the Holy Spirit and walks therein.

> *So I say, walk by the Spirit, and you will not gratify the desires of the flesh.* —**Galatians 5:16 NIV**

THE MINISTRY OF THE HOLY SPIRIT IN THE LIFE OF THE BELIEVER

The baptism of the Holy Spirit takes place at conversion. It is when the Spirit places the new believer in the Body of Christ. 1 Corinthians 12:13 (NKJV) says, "By one Spirit we were all baptized into one body."

According to Ephesians 1:13, the believer is also sealed with the Holy Spirit. To be sealed is to be marked or branded, which shows ownership.

The believer also has the indwelling of the Holy Spirit. 1 Corinthians 6:19 (NKJV) says, "[Do] you not know that your body is the temple of the Holy Spirit who is in you?" Only the believer who is led by the Spirit is filled with the Spirit.

WHAT IS THE SPIRIT-FILLED LIFE?

> *And do not be drunk with wine, in which is dissipation; but be filled with the Spirit.* —**Ephesians 5:18 NKJV**

Paul uses wine to convey the significance of being filled with the Spirit, saying "be not drunk with wine." The root word of intoxicate or intoxication is "toxic," which means poisonous or debilitating.

The New King James Version of the Bible says drunkenness leads to "dissipation." Other versions say, "it leads to debauchery." It is the riotous, reckless, self-destructive life. It cheapens one's life, ultimately destroying one's life.

> *Don't live under the complete control of anything other than the Holy Spirit.*

Order my steps in thy word: and let not any iniquity have dominion over me. —**Psalm 119:133 KJV**

We will never get more of the Holy Spirit. The challenge is for the Holy Spirit to get more of us. The verb "filled" in Ephesians 5:18 means "keep on being filled." It is in the passive voice, which means we do not fill ourselves but permit the Spirit to fill us.

To be filled with the Spirit literally means to be "controlled by." You are controlled by what you submit to. With the exception of the Holy Spirit, we can be destroyed by anything that controls us.

The Spirit-filled life begins with a daily decision. To be filled or controlled by the Spirit requires submission to the Holy Spirit. The evidence of the Spirit-filled life is NOT the gifts of the Spirit, it is the fruit of the Spirit.

WHAT A SPIRIT-FILLED LIFE LOOKS LIKE

While many passages speak to this subject, Ephesians 5 cites the following as marks of the Spirit-filled person:

1. Imitate God (v. 1)
2. Walk in love (v. 2)
3. Live blamelessly (vv. 3–7)
4. Walk as children of light (vv. 8–10)
5. Refrain from unfruitful works of darkness (vv. 11–14)
6. Walk circumspectly (vv. 15–17)
7. Live under the influence of the Holy Spirit (vv. 18–21)

SPIRITS VERSUS THE SPIRIT

Why does Paul juxtapose drunkenness with Spirit-filled living? Have you ever seen a drunk person? Believe it or not, there are a few similarities.

THE SPIRIT-FILLED LIFE

Drunk people are brutally honest. Liquor has been called liquid courage. Once upon a time, Lady Astor said to Winston Churchill, "You are drunk!" Winston Churchill replied, "And you are ugly! Tomorrow I will be sober but you will still be ugly." As the Holy Spirit gives us boldness, Spirit-filled people are yet called upon to "speak the truth in love" (Ephesians 4:15).

Drunk people are often happy. Unfortunately, alcohol-induced happiness is short-lived and may lead to a miserable morning. After all, forty ounces of delight is never enough.

On the other hand, the Spirit-filled person has joy. Joy not only is a fruit of the Spirit, but also is a foretaste of heaven. Pierre de Chardin said, "Joy is the infallible sign of the presence of God."

> *In Your [God's] presence there is fullness of joy.*
> **—Psalm 16:11 NKJV**

Drunk people act abnormally. They may become more enthusiastic, smile or laugh for no reason, become more talkative, and may want to hug everybody—*even perfect strangers!*

Spirit-filled believers are called to do "abnormal" things. The most challenging are perhaps to love their enemies, pray for those who misuse them, and turn the other cheek when offended.

People who are inebriated only do certain things when they are under the influence. The same can be said of born-again believer. We can only live holy lives under the influence of the Holy Spirit.

> *What is this that I feel deep down inside?*
> *What is this that keeps setting my soul on fire?*
> *Whatever it is, it won't let me hold my peace.*
>
> *What is this that makes it seem like I'm acting strange?*
> *What is this that makes me love to call God's Name?*
> *Whatever it is, it won't let me hold my peace.*
>
> *It makes me love my enemies.*
> *It makes me love my friends.*

It won't let me be ashamed to tell the world I've been born again.
Whatever it is, it won't let me hold peace.[3]

What is this?
It is the power of the Holy Spirit.

---

3. "What Is This," Walter Hawkins, (year unknown)

Discussion Questions

1. How would you best characterize the Spirit-filled life?

2. Discuss how each member of the Godhead (Trinity) impacts our lives.

3. Read Galatians 5:16. Describe the tension between the Spirit and the desires of the flesh.

4. Discuss the ministry of the Holy Spirit in the life of the believer.

5. What is the difference between the indwelling of the Holy Spirit and the filling of the Holy Spirit?

6. List seven marks of the Spirit-filled person found in Ephesians 5:

7. Discuss at least three similarities shared by people under the influence of alcohol and people under the influence of the Holy Spirit.

Prayer

Father, thank You for creating us, for redeeming us through the death of Jesus Christ, and for sealing us with Your Holy Spirit. Forgive us for all the times that we were carnal and walked after the flesh. Help us to walk by the Spirit so that we will not gratify the desires of the flesh. Cleanse our hearts so that our bodies are fit to be temples of Your Holy Spirit. Order our steps in Your word and let not any iniquity have dominion over us. In the Name of Jesus Christ, AMEN.

WEEK THREE

MONDAY

TODAY'S VERSES
John 16:12–15

TODAY'S VOICE
Truth does not change, only our awareness of it. —Malcolm X

TODAY'S VICTORY
Pray that the Spirit of truth would guide you into all truth.

TUESDAY

Today's Verses
Galatians 5:13–15

Today's Voice
I've learned that people will forget what you said, people will forget what you did, but people will never forget how you made them feel. —Maya Angelou

Today's Victory
Pray for a mind that does not indulge the flesh but humbly serves others in love.

WEDNESDAY

TODAY'S VERSES
Galatians 5:16–21

TODAY'S VOICE
Lust indulged became habit, and habit unrestrained became necessity. —Saint Augustine

TODAY'S VICTORY
Pray for the will to walk by the Spirit and not gratify the desires of the flesh.

THURSDAY

Today's Verses
Psalm 1

Today's Voice
There comes a point where we need to stop just pulling people out of the river. We need to go upstream and find out why they're falling in. —Desmond Tutu

Today's Victory
Pray that the Holy Spirit would protect you from hearing bad advice and practicing unproductive behaviors.

FRIDAY

Today's Verses
Ephesians 4:14–16

Today's Voice
Whoever debases others is debasing himself. —James Baldwin

Today's Victory
Pray that the Holy Spirit would always lead you to speak the truth in love.

LESSON FOUR

BE IMITATORS OF GOD

"You can love all men perfectly if you love the one God in them all."

MOTHER TERESA

BE IMITATORS OF GOD

Therefore, be imitators of God as dear children. And walk in love, as Christ also has loved us and given Himself for us, an offering and a sacrifice to God for a sweet-smelling aroma.

Ephesians 5:1–2 nkjv

"If the Kingdom of God is in you, you should leave a little bit of heaven wherever you go."

Cornel West

Like many of Paul's epistles, the book of Ephesians emphasizes the connection between doctrine (what we believe) and practice (how we behave). Paul aims to make our theology practical. It is a manual on the Spirit-filled life.

Verse 1 tells us what to do; verse 2 tells us how to do it.

What To Do

Be imitators of God as dear children (**verse 1**).

The Greek word for "follower" or "imitator" is the same as our word "mimic" or "mimeograph." The mimeograph was the precursor to the modern copier. To mimic is to replicate the character or conduct of another person.

Copy the character and conduct of God.

What are *dear* children? The Greek term is *agapetos*. It means "beloved, esteemed, or favorite." Does God actually have favorite children?

YES!

God actually has two sets of children. God has children through creation. God also has children through Christ. Any child of God through creation can enjoy life, but only God's children through Christ can enjoy eternal life.

> *This is eternal life, that they may know You, the only true God, and Jesus Christ whom You have sent.*
> —**John 17:3** NKJV

In Ephesians 1:7 (NKJV), Paul identifies another benefit for God's children through Christ: "We have redemption through His blood, the forgiveness of sins, according to the riches of His grace."

How do we imitate God?

How To Do It

And walk in love… (**verse 2**).

Biblically, to walk literally means "to live." This is the first of three admonitions regarding the believer's walk. Ephesians 5:8 says, "walk as children of light" and verse 15 says "walk circumspectly."

Love should be the ulterior motive of all we do. 1 Corinthians 16:14 (ESV) says, "Let all that you do be done in love."

Love is the character of God manifested in relationship. 1 John 4:16 says, "God is love." Love is the cardinal virtue of the Christian faith.

> *Three things will last forever—faith, hope, and love—and the greatest of these is love.* —**1 Corinthians 13:13** NLT

In the history of the world, more than 35 million laws have been written to enforce ten commandments. In the faith, love is the fulfillment of the law, as Galatians 5:14 (NIV) says, "For the entire law is fulfilled in keeping this one command: 'Love your neighbor as yourself.'"

He who loves another has fulfilled the law.
—**Romans 13:8** NKJV

Love is the ultimate mark and litmus test of discipleship. John 13:35 (NKJV) says, "By this all will know that you are my disciples, if you have love one for another."

A little boy once asked his father, "Daddy, what is a Christian?"

"A born-again believer who loves God and others," said the father.

The boy replied, "Have you ever seen one?"

THE PERFECT EXAMPLE

And walk in love, as Christ also has loved us and given Himself for us, an offering and a sacrifice to God for a sweet-smelling aroma. —**Ephesians 5:2** NKJV

At Calvary, Jesus Christ was both an offering and a sacrifice. What is the difference? In the Old Testament, a sacrifice required blood. An offering requires giving something; a sacrifice requires giving everything.

A chicken and a pig were walking down the road when they saw a sign soliciting donations to feed hungry children.

The chicken said to the pig, "Why don't I donate eggs and you donate ham?"

The pig replied, "For you to donate eggs is an offering but for me to donate ham is a sacrifice!"

At Calvary, Jesus Christ made a sacrificial offering, "a sweet-smelling aroma" that pleased God. The turning point in the believer's life is when he or she begins to live for God's pleasure and not their own.

The greatest example of love took place at Calvary.

THE SPIRIT-FILLED LIFE

At Calvary, the greatest life ever lived, ended with the greatest death ever died, that finished the greatest work ever done! —James Merritt

Greater love has no one than this: to lay down one's life for one's friends. —John 15:13 NIV

Alas! and did my Savior bleed
And did my Sovereign die?
Would He devote that sacred head
For sinners such as I?

At the cross, at the cross where I first saw the light,
And the burden of my heart rolled away,
It was there by faith I received my sight,
And now I am happy all the day!

Was it for crimes that I had done
He groaned upon the tree?
Amazing pity! Grace unknown!
And love beyond degree![4]

---

4. "At the Cross," Isaac Watts (1707)

DISCUSSION QUESTIONS

1. Have you ever seen a mimeograph? If not, look it up and discuss how it might illustrate holiness.

2. How does God have "favorite" children?

3. Read Ephesians 1:7. What are some benefits for children of God through Christ?

4. Define love.

5. What does it mean to "walk in love"?

6. What is the correlation between love and the law?

7. Read John 13:35. Discuss the significance of love in discipleship.

8. What is the difference between a sacrifice and an offering?

PRAYER

Father God, thank You for the privilege to walk intimately with You as Your beloved children. Thank You for demonstrating Your love on Calvary in the death of Your Son, Jesus Christ. Help us to love You wholeheartedly and to love one another as we love ourselves. May the world know that we are Your disciples by our love. In the matchless Name of the Lord Jesus Christ, AMEN.

WEEK FOUR

MONDAY

Today's Verses
John 17:1–5

Today's Voice
Eternal life is not a gift from God; eternal life is the gift OF GOD. —**Oswald Chambers**

Today's Victory
Thank God for eternal life and the privilege to know Jesus Christ intimately.

TUESDAY

TODAY'S VERSES
1 Corinthians 16:13–14

TODAY'S VOICE
Love is a choice we can make every day. —Shonda Rhimes

TODAY'S VICTORY
Pray that the Holy Spirit would govern your motives and that love would be at the center of your words, deeds, and thoughts.

WEDNESDAY

TODAY'S VERSES
John 13:34–35

TODAY'S VOICE
Christianity without discipleship is always Christianity without Christ. —Dietrich Bonhoeffer

TODAY'S VICTORY
Pray that by the Holy Spirit you would model discipleship by loving others.

THURSDAY

TODAY'S VERSES

Romans 13:8–10

TODAY'S VOICE

My humanity is bound up in yours, for we can only be humans together. —**Desmond Tutu**

TODAY'S VICTORY

Pray that the Holy Spirit would help you to love your neighbor as you love yourself and to avoid harming others.

FRIDAY

TODAY'S VERSES
John 15:9–13

TODAY'S VOICE
Jesus died to pay a debt that he did not owe because we owed a debt we could not pay. —Unknown

TODAY'S VICTORY
Thank God for His love demonstrated in the death of Jesus Christ at Calvary.

LESSON FIVE

MATTERS OF MORALITY

*"At the moment I sin, I desire the sin more
than I desire to please God."*

R. C. Sproul

MATTERS OF MORALITY

But fornication and all uncleanness or covetousness, let it not even be named among you, as is fitting for saints; neither filthiness, nor foolish talking, nor coarse jesting, which are not fitting, but rather giving of thanks. For this you know, that no fornicator, unclean person, nor covetous man, who is an idolater, has any inheritance in the kingdom of Christ and God. Let no one deceive you with empty words, for because of these things the wrath of God comes upon the sons of disobedience. Therefore do not be partakers with them. For you were once darkness, but now you are light in the Lord. Walk as children of light.

EPHESIANS 5:3–8 NKJV

When D. L. Moody heard someone say, "The world has yet to see what God can do with one man fully surrendered to Him," Moody purposed in his heart, "By God's grace, I'll be that man!"

To fear God simply means to take God seriously, as opposed to taking God casually. — **Tony Evans**

The Spirit-filled life requires complete surrender to God. It is reflected in moral conduct, conversation, and companions. What we do, what we say, and who we spend time with says a lot about us.

THE SPIRIT-FILLED LIFE IS REFLECTED IN MORAL CONDUCT.

Fornication and all uncleanness or covetousness, let it not even be named among you, as is fitting for saints (**verse 3**).

SEXUAL IMMORALITY

The sexual revolution was actually a rebellion. It was the deconstruction of biblical convictions regarding human sexuality. Society perpetuated the myth of safe sex to avoid babies and diseases. It may also prevent intimacy. While love validates us, lust violates us.

There is no such thing as safe sex. Pills, procedures, and prophylactics cannot prevent emotionally transmitted diseases. However, there is "sacred" sex, which can only be found within the context of marriage.

Marriage is honorable among all, and the bed undefiled.
—Hebrews 13:4 NKJV

Anything and everything else is sin!

The late radio personality Paul Harvey told the story of how an Eskimo kills a wolf. It speaks to the overwhelming, self-destructive nature of sin—particularly sexual immorality.

The Eskimo coats the blade of a knife with animal blood and allows it to freeze. He repeats this process, adding several layers of frozen blood until the blade of the knife is completely hidden by the frozen blood.

The hunter then fixes the knife in the ground with only the blood-covered blade visible. The wolf will follow its sensitive nose to the bloody knife. While the wolf enjoys the frozen blood, it doesn't notice the sting of the razor-sharp blade on his tongue.

The wolf also fails to recognize the instant at which its insatiable thirst is being satisfied by its own blood. The wolf's unrestrained appetite for more ultimately leads to its death.

The wolf literally enjoys its own demise.

Temptation comes from our own desires, which entice us and drag us away. These desires give birth to sinful actions. And when sin is allowed to grow, it gives birth to death.
—James 1:14–15 NLT

IMPURITY

In our lifetime, sin has become normative. Guilt and shame are things of the past. Morality is now relative. We have no spiritual orientation. Like the children of Israel in the book of Judges, "everyone is doing what is right in their own eyes."

We have grown nose-blind to the stench of sin in our society.

A college football team used a goat as their mascot. A couple of players offered to keep the goat in their dorm room.
The coach asked, "What about the smell?"
The players replied, "He'll get used to it!"

But know this, that in the last days perilous times will come: For men will be lovers of themselves, lovers of money, boasters, proud, blasphemers, disobedient to parents, unthankful, unholy, unloving, unforgiving, slanderers, without self-control, brutal, despisers of good, traitors, headstrong, haughty, lovers of pleasure rather than lovers of God, having a form of godliness but denying its power. And from such people turn away! —**2 Timothy 3:1–5** NKJV

COVETOUSNESS (IDOLATRY)

Prader-Willi Syndrome is a complex genetic disorder. One of its symptoms is perpetual hunger due to the inability to feel full or satisfied. For most of us, the problem isn't food but our unappeasable appetite for things. Our mantra is the 1965 words of the Rolling Stones: "I can't get no satisfaction."

Covetousness or greed is the inordinate quest of more—at any cost! The covetous man never has enough. He is consumed by want. He is a slave to "more." The covetous man never gains the whole world but may lose his soul trying.

At least twice, Paul likens covetousness to idolatry. Greed is idolatrous because it rejects God in pursuit of what only God can provide. Greed puts things in the place of God. Jesus said, "No one can serve two masters. ... You cannot serve both God and money" (Matthew 6:24 NIV).

> *Money is like salt water. The more a man drinks the thirstier he becomes.* —**Roman proverb**

A Warning

For this you know, that no fornicator, unclean person, nor covetous man, who is an idolater, has any inheritance in the kingdom of Christ and God (**verse 5**).

The Spirit-filled life is reflected in moral conversation.

Neither filthiness, nor foolish talking, nor coarse jesting, which are not fitting, but rather giving of thanks (**verse 4**).

Filthiness in this context refers to language that dishonors God, others, and even oneself. "Coarse jesting" is crude, vulgar humor. Paul also discourages "foolish talk." The wise man has something to say; the fool has to say something.

We are not sure who first said, "Better to remain silent and be thought a fool than to speak and remove all doubt." However, Proverbs 17:28 (NIV) says, "Even fools are thought wise if they keep silent."

Your language reflects your lifestyle. A person who will say anything just might do anything. A filthy mouth is a sign of a filthy mind. Matthew 15:18 implies that whatever comes out of your mouth comes out of your heart.

Eleanor Roosevelt said, "Great minds discuss ideas; average minds discuss events; small minds discuss people." People run their mouths when they have nothing else to run. How interesting it is that we have tamed tigers but cannot tame the tongue.

Thanksgiving is the cure for gossip!

THE SPIRIT-FILLED LIFE IS REFLECTED IN MORAL COMPANIONS.

Let no one deceive you with empty words, for because of these things the wrath of God comes upon the sons of disobedience. Therefore do not be partakers with them. For you were once darkness, but now you are light in the Lord. Walk as children of light (**verses 6–8**).

Be careful who you listen to. Do not be deceived by vain words, philosophical arguments, or empty and illusive doctrines. If it is new, it may not be true; however, if it is true, it is not new.

Be careful whom you hang with. Paul emphatically says, "Do not be partakers" with "the sons of disobedience." You will eventually become the sum total of the people you hang out with. Maybe your child hangs with "them" because they are one of "them."

Bad company corrupts good character.
—1 Corinthians 15:33 NIV

It is better to be alone than in bad company.
—**Booker T. Washington**

ARE THE PEOPLE IN YOUR CIRCLE ASSETS OR LIABILITIES?

One day a farmer grabbed his shotgun to get rid of a flock of annoying crows. Unfortunately, he did not see his parrot in the pack. When his children saw the slain birds, they asked, "What happened to the parrot?" The farmer simply replied, "Bad company!"

THE SPIRIT-FILLED LIFE

MORAL OF THE STORY:

Don't ever become the collateral damage of somebody else's foolishness.

He who walks with wise men will be wise, but the companion of fools will be destroyed. —**Proverbs 13:20** NIV

DISCUSSION QUESTIONS

1. Discuss how the Spirit-filled life is reflected in our moral conduct.

2. Why is holiness important?

3. How have we become "nose-blind" to sin in recent generations?

4. Define covetousness. How does it affect our lives?

5. Read Matthew 15:18. What is the correlation between our language and our lifestyles?

6. Describe the value of good company.

7. Elaborate on how you select friends.

Prayer

Heavenly Father, we know that You have called us to be holy as You are holy. Forgive our sins and deliver us from the strongholds that handicap our lives. Guard our tongues so that our speech honors You. Give us the wisdom to select godly friends who make us better and inspire us to walk more intimately with You. In the mighty and matchless Name of the Lord Jesus Christ, AMEN.

WEEK FIVE

MONDAY

Today's Verses
1 Peter 1:13–16

Today's Voice
The holier a man becomes, the more he mourns over the unholiness which remains in him. —C. S. Lewis

Today's Victory
Pray that the Holy Spirit would sanctify your conduct to reflect the character of God.

TUESDAY

TODAY'S VERSES
Psalm 139:23–24

TODAY'S VOICE
Even our tears of repentance need to be washed in the blood of the Lamb. —**Jerry Bridges**

TODAY'S VICTORY
Pray that the Holy Spirit would reveal your anxieties and offensive ways and lead you in the path of righteousness.

WEDNESDAY

Today's Verses
James 1:13–15

Today's Voice
Temptation is not a sin but playing with temptation invited sin. —Fulton Sheen

Today's Victory
Pray that the Holy Spirit would lead and guide you when facing temptation.

THURSDAY

Today's Verses
Romans 12:1–2

Today's Voice
Holiness, not happiness, is the chief end of man. —Oswald Chambers

Today's Victory
Pray for a heart to present yourself to God as a living sacrifice and that the Holy Spirit would transform your mind.

FRIDAY

Today's Verse
2 Corinthians 7:1

Today's Voice
My life is such a contradiction. My soul yearns for holiness and then runs from the mortification necessary to attain it. —Mother Angelica

Today's Victory
Pray that the Holy Spirit would cleanse you from sin and perfect you out of reverence for God.

CHILDREN OF THE LIGHT

"To examine whether your heart pleases Him is not necessary, but rather whether His Heart pleases you."

St Francis de Sales

CHILDREN OF THE LIGHT

For you were once darkness, but now you are light in the Lord. Live as children of light (for the fruit of the light consists in all goodness, righteousness and truth) and find out what pleases the Lord.

EPHESIANS 5:8–10 NIV

"All the darkness in the world cannot extinguish the light of a single candle."

SAINT FRANCIS OF ASSISI

LIGHT VERSUS DARKNESS

Ancient thought used light and darkness metaphorically for good and evil. Verse 8 cites both what we were and what we are. We were "darkness" but now we are "light in the Lord."

Darkness is the natural state of humanity. Proverbs 4:19 (NKJV) says, "The way of the wicked is like darkness." Jesus said in John 3:19 (NKJV), "Men loved darkness rather than light, because their deeds were evil." As light and darkness cannot coexist, the difference between what we were and what we are is the grace of God.

We can easily forgive a child who is afraid of the dark; the real tragedy of life is when men are afraid of the light.
— **Plato**

WALK AS CHILDREN OF LIGHT

Jesus identified his disciples as "the light of the world." Thus, we cannot blend in and stand out at the same time. As 1 John 1:5 says,

"God is light," so believers are called to reflect God's character in the world.

It took Leonardo da Vinci three years to finish his masterpiece *The Last Supper*. He asked a friend to critique the painting.

"It's wonderful!" exclaimed the friend. "The cup is so real I cannot divert my eyes from it!"

Leonardo immediately took a brush and painted over that gorgeous, magnificent cup and said, "Nothing shall detract from the figure of Christ!"

> *Let your light so shine before men, that they may see your good works and glorify your Father in heaven.*
> —**Matthew 5:16 NKJV**

> *This little light of mine,*
> *I'm going to let it shine.*
>
> *Everywhere I go,*
> *I'm going to let it shine.*
>
> *In my neighbor's home,*
> *I'm going to let it shine.*
>
> *Shine!*
> *Shine!*
> *Shine!*[5]

What does it mean to walk as "children of light?" Paul cites three things that he refers to as "the fruit of the light."

Goodness—the right character

A young lady brought her new boyfriend home to meet her family. She asked her grandmother, "Isn't he cute?" Her grandmother replied, "I don't know. I haven't seen him on the inside yet."

---

5. Origin unknown

> *Outer beauty captures the eye;*
> *inner beauty captures the heart.*

Apart from the image of God, the atoning work of the Lord Jesus Christ, and the indwelling presence of the Holy Spirit, there is no good in us. Jesus said, "No one is good except God alone" (Mark 10:18 NIV).

HOW CAN WE BE GOOD IF WE ARE INHERENTLY SINFUL?

Therefore, if anyone is in Christ, he is a new creation; old things have passed away; behold, all things have become new. —**2 Corinthians 5:17 NKJV**

Righteousness — the right conduct

Conduct follows character. It is not enough to clean our hands; we also must clean our hearts. What we do reflects who we are. For example, a liar lies. A thief steals. You cannot blame a dog for barking. It's what dogs do!

RIGHTEOUSNESS IS ALWAYS RIGHT!

It is never right to do wrong, and it is never wrong to do right. It doesn't matter what's legal or socially acceptable. It doesn't matter what the Supreme Court says. It doesn't matter what the majority says nor what the masses do. It doesn't matter what feels good or what we believe. Righteousness is ALWAYS right, and God's children are called to be holy!

> *Righteousness exalts a nation, but sin is a reproach to any people.* —**Proverbs 14:34 NKJV**

> *If there is righteousness in the heart, there will be beauty in the character. If there is beauty in the character, there*

THE SPIRIT-FILLED LIFE

will be harmony in the home. If there is harmony in the home, there will be order in the nation. If there is order in the nation, there will be peace in the world.
—**Chinese proverb**

Whoever pursues righteousness and love finds life, prosperity and honor. —**Proverbs 21:21 NIV**

Blessed are they which do hunger and thirst after righteousness: for they shall be filled. —**Matthew 5:6 KJV**

Truth—the right convictions

The administration of a recent past president was driven by "alternative facts." That president's personal attorney even said, "Truth is not truth." Another former president said, "It depends on what your meaning of the word 'is' is."

It has been said that there are three things that cannot be hidden for long: the sun, the moon, and the truth. When you tell the truth you don't have to remember what you said. The problem with a half-truth is you may have gotten the wrong half.

Lies fly but they have no legs to stand on when they get there. —**Unknown**

Be true to yourself. When you are true, you can survive what is not. There is no substitute for authenticity. The worst lies are the ones we tell ourselves. You cannot change the truth, but the truth can change you. Jesus said, "The truth will set you free."

Your word I have hidden in my heart that I might not sin against You. —**Psalm 119:11 NKJV**

Your word is a lamp for my feet, a light on my path.
—**Psalm 119:105 NIV**

Order my steps in thy word, and let not any iniquity have dominion over me. —Psalm 119:133 KJV

LIVE TO PLEASE THE LORD

[Find] out what is acceptable to the Lord (**verse 10**).

As the spirit and the flesh are constantly at war, Romans 8:8 (NKJV) says, "Those who are in the flesh cannot please God." The turning point in the believer's life is the decision to please God rather than oneself. There are at least five things in Scripture that please the Lord:

1. Faith

Without faith it is impossible to please God.
—Hebrews 11:6 NIV

Faith is not just believing in God—even demons do that. Faith is believing God. It has been said that believing in God will take you to heaven; however, believing God will bring heaven to you.

2. Fearing the Lord

The LORD takes pleasure in those who fear Him.
—Psalm 147:11 NKJV

To fear God is to live in awe and reverence of God. It is to respect God's personality (who God is), power (what God does), and prerogatives (what God chooses).

3. Walking intimately with God

Hebrews 11:5 says Enoch had this testimony: "He pleased God." While we know very little about him, Genesis 5:24 says, "Enoch walked with God." Colossians 1:10 says that walking worthy of the Lord pleases Him.

4. Blessing God and others

Hebrews 13:15–16 (NKJV) encourages that in addition to offering "the sacrifice of praise to God," we should not forget to do good and to share with those in need, "for with such sacrifices God is well pleased" (verse 16).

5. Submission to God's will

The Bible says obedience is better than sacrifice (1 Samuel 15:22). The first thing God wants from us is us, the gift of ourselves. Romans 12:1 (NKJV) says, "Present your bodies a living sacrifice, holy, acceptable to God, which is your reasonable service."

While it is our aim to please God, Saint Francis de Sales took a different approach: "To examine whether your heart pleases Him is not necessary, but rather whether His Heart pleases you." In other words, our hearts can only be content when God's heart is.

> *Delight yourself also in the LORD, And He shall give you the desires of your heart.* —**Psalm 37:4** NKJV

DISCUSSION QUESTIONS

1. Describe the darkness of sin.

2. What does it mean to walk as "children of light"?

3. Read Matthew 5:16. How should our lights ultimately bring glory to God?

4. According to the New International Version of the Bible, what are the three "fruit of the light" that Paul cites in Ephesians 5:9? Elaborate on each.

THE SPIRIT-FILLED LIFE

5. Read Proverbs 21:21. Discuss the blessings and benefits in pursuing righteousness and love.

6. Identify at least three popular lies that we tell ourselves.

7. Why is it important to please God?

8. Discuss the five things that please the Lord in Scripture.

PRAYER

God, thank You for delivering us from darkness and bringing us into the light. Forgive us for all the times that we yet loved darkness rather than light. Help us to walk as children of light and to let our lights shine before the world. May our lives reflect goodness, righteousness, and truth. Deliver us from the flesh wherein we cannot please You, but help us to honor You in word, in deed, and in thought. In the Name of Jesus, AMEN.

WEEK SIX

MONDAY

Today's Verses
1 John 1:5–7

Today's Voice
Everyone is a moon, and has a dark side which he never shows to anybody. —Mark Twain

Today's Victory
Pray that God would deliver you from any area of darkness that may be in your life and that the Holy Spirit would enable you to walk in the light.

TUESDAY

Today's Verses
Matthew 5:13–16

Today's Voice
Character is power. —Booker T. Washington

Today's Victory
Pray that the Holy Spirit would radiate in your life as the salt of the earth and the light of the world to the glory of God.

WEDNESDAY

Today's Verses

John 1:1–5, 14
Psalm 119:133

Today's Voice

The truth is like a lion; you don't have to defend it. Let it loose; it will defend itself. —Saint Augustine

Today's Victory

Pray that the Holy Spirit would order your steps in the Word and prevent any iniquity from having dominion over your life.

THURSDAY

TODAY'S VERSES
Romans 8:1–8

TODAY'S VOICE
I serve God, and my purpose is to please Him, and if God be for you, who can be against you? —**Ben Carson**

TODAY'S VICTORY
Pray for a heart to walk after the Spirit (not the flesh) and a mind to please God.

FRIDAY

TODAY'S VERSES
John 8:31–32

TODAY'S VOICE
Truth is powerful and it prevails. —Sojourner Truth

TODAY'S VICTORY
Pray that the Holy Spirit would help you abide in the Word, reveal and guide you into all truth, and set you free from any bondage that you may be subject to.

LESSON SEVEN

FRUITLESS DEEDS OF DARKNESS

"Hope is being able to see that there is light despite all of the darkness."

Desmond Tutu

FRUITLESS DEEDS OF DARKNESS

Have nothing to do with the fruitless deeds of darkness, but rather expose them. It is shameful even to mention what the disobedient do in secret. But everything exposed by the light becomes visible and everything that is illuminated becomes a light. This is why it is said: "Wake up, sleeper, rise from the dead, and Christ will shine on you."

Ephesians 5:11–14 niv

"Darkness cannot drive out darkness: only light can do that. Hate cannot drive out hate: only love can do that."

Martin Luther King Jr.

Light versus Darkness

Verses 11 through 14 conclude a thought that began in verse 8. It cites both what we were and what we are. We were "darkness," but now we are "light in the Lord." Paul encourages us to "walk as children of the light," which produces goodness, righteousness, and truth.

Do Not Participate!

Have no fellowship with the unfruitful works of darkness (verse 11 kjv).

How ironic it is that the King James Version of the Bible uses the word "fellowship." The Greek term means to share company and/or conduct. The company that you keep can impact the character that you develop. It is always easier to get into trouble than it is to get out.

The people closest to you should not just be happy, healthy, and holy, they should inspire you to be happy, healthy, and holy. Your better friends are the ones that make you better. Remember: *Happy people may not necessarily make you happy, but sick people can make you sick!*

Every Joshua needs a Moses,
and every Moses needs a Joshua.

The "Moses" in your life is the person who inspires you. The "Joshua" in your life is the person that you inspire. Give your "Joshua" everything that your "Moses" gave you.

Fruitless Deeds of Darkness

Have nothing to do with the fruitless deeds of darkness,
but rather expose them (**verse 11 NIV**).

At the end of the day, what have you gained from your dark deeds? We are not sure if sin pays, but it definitely costs! There is an overwhelming distinction between value and price. A new car loses a large percentage of its value as soon as it is driven off the lot.

As with the purchase of a new car, the value of a sin drops as soon as the deal is done! You will always pay too much for too little! Sin is overrated and overpriced. At the end of the day, sin is NEVER worth it!

The Western Roman Empire fell in 476 CE. At least the next five centuries were known as the Dark Ages. As Scripture uses darkness to metaphorically describe ignorance, evil, and even the rejection of Christ, we must ask:

Are we living in the Dark Ages?

But know this, that in the last days perilous times will come:
For men will be lovers of themselves, lovers of money, boasters, proud, blasphemers, disobedient to parents, unthankful, unholy, unloving, unforgiving, slanderers, without

self-control, brutal, despisers of good, traitors, headstrong, haughty, lovers of pleasure rather than lovers of God, having a form of godliness but denying its power. And from such people turn away! —2 Timothy 3:1–5 NKJV

EXPOSE THEM!

While Paul admonishes us to have nothing to do with fruitless deeds of darkness, he commands us to "expose them." Perhaps, the greatest tragedy of our times is the normalization of sin. We have not exposed sin; we have excused sin.

In his book entitled *Whatever Became of Sin?*, Karl Menninger warned against relegating sin to mere symptoms. For example, the Bible calls pride a sin, not a symptom of a narcissistic personality disorder.

Today mental illness covers a multitude of sins. However, you cannot fix morality with medication. In contemporary culture, everyone is a victim, but no one is a sinner. Why? Because victims are not responsible for what they do.

It is necessary to expose sin so that people will know what sin is. How do we expose them? Simply turn on the light. People who work in banks can spot counterfeit money because they have been trained to recognize real money. If a child grows up and only sees alcoholics, that child may not know drunkenness is a sin.

> *It is shameful even to mention what the disobedient do in secret. But everything exposed by the light becomes visible and everything that is illuminated becomes a light* (**verses 12–13** NIV).

> *Look at how a single candle can both defy and define the darkness.* —**Anne Frank**

BEWARE OF YOUR OWN SINS!
Expose deeds, not people!

It is ours to destroy sin, not sinners. While we are called to be witnesses, we have too many judges. Jesus said, "Judge not, that you be not judged" (Matthew 7:1 NKJV). The problem with those who wish to judge is they compare what is bad in others to what is good in them.

Jesus Christ is the standard, and we are not.

Wake up, sleeper, rise from the dead, and Christ will shine on you (**verse 14 NIV**).

Then Jesus spoke to them again, saying, "I am the light of the world. He who follows Me shall not walk in darkness, but have the light of life." —**John 8:12 NKJV**

An interesting thing happened in Chicago on March 19, 2015. A building went up in flames in the 4000 block of South Pulaski Road near I-55. It took 156 firefighters and 26 pieces of equipment to put out the three-alarm fire.

What is ironic is the building was occupied by a business that manufactured fire extinguishers. A company that manufactured fire extinguishers made no provision for putting out its own fire.

If someone is caught in a sin, you who live by the Spirit should restore that person gently. But watch yourselves, or you also may be tempted. —**Galatians 6:1 NIV**

The story is told of a blind man who carried a lantern. When asked why he carried a lantern despite the fact that he could not see, he replied, "I don't want anyone to stumble over me."

DISCUSSION QUESTIONS

1. How does one move from darkness to light?

2. Why are we discouraged from fellowship with darkness?

3. Describe ideal friends.

4. What can we learn from the relationship between Moses and Joshua?

5. Read 2 Timothy 3:1–5. Are we living in the Dark Ages? Elaborate.

6. How has sin become normalized?

7. What does it mean to expose sin?

8. How can we condemn sin without condemning people?

9. Read John 8:12 and discuss Jesus Christ as the Light of the World.

10. What is the appropriate way to handle someone caught in a sin?

PRAYER

Dear Lord, forgive us for our partnership in unfruitful works of darkness. We are terribly ashamed of our disobedience. At the end of the day, we had absolutely nothing to gain by such. Deliver us from what appears to be the spiritual Dark Ages. Help us to expose sin in our world and restore sinners gently. May we always beware of our own sins so that we will neither stumble nor cause others to do so. In the Name of Jesus, AMEN.

WEEK SEVEN

MONDAY

TODAY'S VERSES
Romans 10:1–13

TODAY'S VOICE
And I was in darkness so darkness I became. —Anonymous

TODAY'S VICTORY
Ask God to forgive us for ignoring His righteousness and going about to establish our own.

TUESDAY

TODAY'S VERSES
Colossians 1:9–13

TODAY'S VOICE

Forgiveness is the fragrance the flower releases on the foot that has crushed it. —Mark Twain

TODAY'S VICTORY

Thank God for rescuing us from the dominion of darkness and for forgiving our sins.

WEDNESDAY

TODAY'S VERSES

1 Thessalonians 5:5–11

TODAY'S VOICE

Our greatest glory is not in never failing, but in rising up every time we fail. —Ralph Waldo Emerson

TODAY'S VICTORY

Pray for self-control and for your life to reflect faith, love, and the hope of our salvation.

THURSDAY

Today's Verses
Romans 13:11–14

Today's Voice
Give light, and people will find the way. —Ella Baker

Today's Victory
Pray that the Holy Spirit would enable us to cast off the works of darkness and put on the armor of light.

FRIDAY

Today's Verses
John 3:16–21

Today's Voice
Let nothing dim the light that shines from within. —Maya Angelou

Today's Victory
Thank God for the sacrifice of His Son, Jesus Christ, for our sins and pray for a heart that loves light rather than darkness.

LESSON EIGHT

WALK CIRCUMSPECTLY

"We are 100 percent responsible for the pursuit of holiness, but at the same time we are 100 percent dependent upon the Holy Spirit to enable us in that pursuit. The pursuit of holiness is not a pull-yourself-up-by-your-own-bootstraps approach to the Christian life."

JERRY BRIDGES

WALK CIRCUMSPECTLY

See then that you walk circumspectly, not as fools but as wise, redeeming the time, because the days are evil. Therefore do not be unwise, but understand what the will of the Lord is.

Ephesians 5:15–17 nkjv

"Everybody wants confidence, but you do not find it in self-help books. You find confidence in the Holy Spirit."

Rick Warren

A man and his son went to a particular town looking for an uncle that they had never seen. Suddenly, the father saw a man from a significant distance and exclaimed, "There goes my uncle!"

His son asked, "How do you know that's your uncle when you have never seen him before?"

The man replied, "Son, he has to be my uncle because he walks exactly like my father."

The Holy Spirit works in our lives to conform us to the image and likeness of God. Romans 8:16 (nkjv) says, "The Spirit Himself bears witness with our spirit that we are children of God."

It's in the Walk!

The Spirit-filled life requires walking in love (verse 2). Love is the ultimate mark of discipleship. John 13:35 (kjv) says, "By this shall all men know that ye are my disciples, if ye have love one to another."

The Spirit-filled life requires walking as children of light (verse 8). This produces three fruits: goodness, righteousness, and truth (verse 9). Jesus Christ even identified his disciples as "the light of the word."

The Spirit-filled life requires walking circumspectly (verse 15). This means to walk carefully, as the wise person cautiously considers the consequences of their conduct.

> *Ancient man was preoccupied with how to be good and modern man is preoccupied with how to be happy.*
> —**Dr. Peter Kreeft**

FOOLISHNESS VERSUS WISDOM

In Jesus' parable of the builders, the wise man built his house on a rock while the foolish man built his house on sand. The wise build on the solid; the foolish build on the superficial. When the storm came, the house built on the rock survived; the house built on sand did not.

> *But everyone who hears these words of mine and does not put them into practice is like a foolish man who built his house on sand.* —**Matthew 7:26** NIV

The book of Proverbs makes at least ten distinctions between the wise and the foolish.

> *The wise brings joy to the father.*
> *The foolish brings grief to the mother.*
>
> *The wise choose wise friends.*
> *The foolish choose foolish friends.*
>
> *The wise inherit honor.*
> *The foolish inherit shame.*
>
> *The wise avoid danger.*
> *The foolish approach danger.*

The wise listen first.
The foolish speak first.

The way of a fool is right in his own eyes, But he who heeds counsel is wise. —**Proverbs 12:15** NKJV

What It Means To "Redeem the Time"

The term "redeem" means to buy back or regain possession of something. This phrase obviously does not have reference to the past in that time is an element that we cannot recover. We should not just count the time; we should make the time count.

We all have moments that we wish we could buy back!

To "redeem the time" means to maximize every moment. The New International Version of the Bible renders it "make the most of every opportunity." It is not to mourn the time lost but to make the best of the time left. The goal is not to count moments but to make moments count!

How to determine how to spend your time:

1. Is it worth the investment?

Time is more valuable than money. While you can earn more money, you cannot earn more time. It has been said that there are at least four things that you cannot recover:

the stone after it is cast,
the word after it is said,
the occasion after it is missed, and
the time after it is gone.

2. Does it have eternal significance?

Make the moment greater than the minute. Reading a book is a good thing. Reading a book to a child is a great thing. Great people plant trees knowing that they may not live long enough to enjoy the shade. Always ask, will it matter tomorrow?

3. Does it bring glory to God or good to others?
The person who blesses God and others shall be blessed.

> *Delight yourself also in the LORD, And He shall give you the desires of your heart.* —**Psalm 37:4** NKJV

> *A generous person will prosper; whoever refreshes others will be refreshed.* —**Proverbs 11:25** NIV

UNDERSTAND THE WILL OF GOD

Therefore do not be unwise, but understand what the will of the Lord is (**verse 17**).

The Spirit-filled life is not a spiritual "entanglement." God does not wish to be a friend extending benefits in the absence of a commitment to an exclusive relationship. The Spirit-filled life is not a Sunday morning rendezvous to compensate for six days of spiritual neglect.

> *The will of God demands complete commitment.*

> *I beseech you therefore, brethren, by the mercies of God, that you present your bodies a living sacrifice, holy, acceptable to God, which is your reasonable service. And do not be conformed to this world, but be transformed by the renewing of your mind, that you may prove what is that good and acceptable and perfect will of God.*
> —**Romans 12:1–2** NKJV

> *The safest place to be is in the will of God. Someone said, "The will of God is a soft pillow."*

Disney World has been called "the happiest place on earth." There are several problems with that. First, not everyone can afford the cost of admission. The park closes at a certain hour. Besides memories and souvenirs, you cannot take the Disney experience out of the park.

The happiest place on earth is not Disney World. The happiest place in the world is the kingdom of God and the will of God. It is the human heart that finds its delight in the Lord.

> *Delight yourself in the LORD, and he will give you the desires of your heart.* —Psalm 37:4 ESV

A Mantra to Live By

The Will of God -
Nothing more,
Nothing less,
Nothing else.

F. E. MARSH

Have Thine own way, Lord!
Have Thine own way!
Thou art the potter,
I am the clay!

Mold me and make me
After Thy will,
While I am waiting,
Yielded and still.[6]

---

6. "Have Thine Own Way, Lord," Adelaide Pollard (1906)

DISCUSSION QUESTIONS

1. What does it mean to walk circumspectly?

2. Read Matthew 7:26. How does Jesus distinguish between the foolish and the wise?

3. Discuss distinctions made between the foolish and the wise in the book of Proverbs.

4. How can we redeem the time?

5. Describe the evil in our times.

6. Elaborate on how you determine how to spend your time.

7. How can we understand God's will for our lives?

8. Reflect on the mantra below:

> *The Will of God -*
> *Nothing more,*
> *Nothing less,*
> *Nothing else.*
>
> F. E. MARSH

THE SPIRIT-FILLED LIFE

PRAYER

God, You are calling us to walk in love, in light, and in wisdom. May we reflect Your glory in all that we say, think, and do. Help us to redeem the time by making the most of every moment. Give us the strength and courage to make the rest of our days the best of our days. Make Your will clear to us so that we can live according to eternal significance. In the Name of Jesus Christ, Amen.

WEEK EIGHT

MONDAY

TODAY'S VERSES
James 1:2–8

TODAY'S VOICE
It's not the load that breaks you down, it's the way you carry it. —Lena Horne

TODAY'S VICTORY
Ask God for wisdom to govern your life.

TUESDAY

Today's Verses
Proverbs 3:13–18

Today's Voice
The will of God can always be found in the Word of God.
—E. K. Bailey

Today's Victory
Surrender your mind to the mind of God and embrace wisdom as a tree of life.

WEDNESDAY

Today's Verses
Mark 7:20–23

Today's Voice
God has promised forgiveness to your repentance, but He has not promised tomorrow to your procrastination.
—Saint Augustine

Today's Victory
Confess any sin that may be in your life and ask God to cleanse your heart.

THURSDAY

Today's Verses
Hebrews 12:7–11

Today's Voice
The awareness of being a child of God tends to stabilize the ego and results in a new courage, fearlessness, and power.
— Howard Thurman

Today's Victory
Pray for the mind to accept discipline as an expression of God's love.

FRIDAY

Today's Verses
Galatians 6:7–10

Today's Voice
Now the only way you can serve God on earth is by serving others. —Rick Warren

Today's Victory
Pray for a heart to do good to others, especially other believers.

EPILOGUE

MARKS OF MATURITY

The goal of this command is love, which comes from a pure heart and a good conscience and a sincere faith.

1 Timothy 1:5 niv

What's Love Got To Do with It?

The Body of Christ has never been without false teachers. Throughout his epistles, Paul consistently confronted erroneous doctrines. In 1 Timothy 1, Paul charged Timothy to restrict certain people from teaching in that they only cause disputes rather than edification in the faith. Paul further established love as the goal of Timothy's pastoral ministry, saying, "The goal of this command is love" (verse 5).

Love is not just the motive behind ministry, "love is the fulfillment of the law" (Romans 13:10 niv). Love is the ultimate mark of a disciple.

> *A new command I give you: Love one another. As I have loved you, so you must love one another. By this everyone will know that you are my disciples, if you love one another.*
> —John 13:34–35 niv

Disciples love God with the totality of their being—heart, mind, soul, and strength (Luke 10:27). Disciples love others as they love themselves, and the most mature disciples even love their enemies.

According to 1 Timothy 1:5, love is the result of three marks of spiritual maturity: a pure heart, a good conscience, and a sincere faith.

A PURE HEART

There are at least three biblical concepts that are no longer widely embraced. They are holiness, sin, and repentance. At best, holiness now describes charismatic denominations, sin is thought to be relative, and repentance is unnecessary because nobody is ever wrong.

How did we get here?

The contemporary curse of humanity is that we no longer fear God. Even when we embrace God's love, faithfulness, mercy, and grace, we tend to avoid God's holiness because it makes demands on our character.

For God did not call us to be impure, but to live a holy life.
—1 Thessalonians 4:7 NIV

It has been said that the heart of the problem is the problem of the heart. "Out of the heart come evil thoughts, murder, adultery, sexual immorality, theft, false testimony, slander" (Matthew 15:19 NIV).
In the Beatitudes, Jesus said, "Blessed are the pure in heart, for they shall see God" (Matthew 5:8 ESV). C. S. Lewis adds, "Only the pure in heart will see God because only the pure in heart want to."

[God] chose us in him before the creation of the world to be holy and blameless in his sight. —Ephesians 1:4 NIV

Holiness is the reflection of God's character in the life of the believer. The nineteenth-century Scottish theologian John Brown said, "Holiness is thinking as God thinks, and willing as God wills." Hebrews 12:14 (NIV) says, "Without holiness no one will see the Lord."

In the forests of northern Europe and Asia lives a little animal called the ermine. It is known for its snow-white fur in winter. The ermine instinctively protects his white coat against anything that would soil it AT ALL COSTS!

Fur hunters have a unique way to capture ermine. They find the ermine's home, usually a cleft in a rock or a hollow in an old tree, and smear the entrance with filth, grime, or dirt. The hunters set their dogs to chase them, knowing they will retreat to their homes.

The ermine will not enter a filthy home. It is captured because the ermine would rather die than be dirty. For the ermine, purity is more precious than life.

> *Order my steps in thy word: and let not any iniquity have dominion over me.* —**Psalm 119:133 KJV**

A Good Conscience

In the song "Running Out of Lies," blues singer Johnny Taylor said, "I made a deal with my conscience; that if my conscience didn't bother me, I sure wouldn't bother my conscience." However, it does not work that way!

> *The conscience is a thousand witnesses.* —**Unknown**

The conscience is a gift from God. At the core of one's self-awareness, the conscience provides a sense of right and wrong. It is a moral compass and a mechanism of self-critique and self-control. The eighteenth-century Polish king Stanisław Leszczyński said, "[The] conscience warns us as a friend before it punishes us as a judge."

A young man worked as a salesclerk in a store that sold fine silk to people of the upper classes in London. One day his employer showed him how he could increase sales and profits by subtly stretching the silk as he measured it out.

The young man looked his employer straight in the eye and said, "Sir, your silk may stretch but my conscience won't."

> *He who sacrifices his conscience to ambition, burns a picture to obtain the ashes.* —**Chinese proverb**

Throughout the history of mankind, people groups, even those without a formal religious system, have always recognized values that prescribed ethical behavior. Thus, everyone has a conscience. According to 1 Timothy 1:19, some have silenced their consciences. This is like removing the battery from a fire detector to silence the beeping versus replacing the weak battery. You have peace but no protection.

It is also possible to have a seared conscience. This occurs when people ignore God so much that they no longer hear Him. Thus, they are insensitive to His Word. Their habits then rule their hearts. 1 Timothy 4:2 (MSG) says, "They've lost their capacity for truth."

> *A bad conscience is a snake in one's heart.*
> —**Jewish proverb**

A good conscience is a clear conscience, and a clear conscience is a clean conscience. The conscience of the believer is cleansed by the blood of Jesus Christ (Hebrews 9:14). The believer keeps his or her conscience clear by yielding to the Word of God and the work of the Holy Spirit.

> *Thy word have I hid in mine heart, that I might not sin against thee.* —**Psalm 119:11** KJV

> *There is therefore now no condemnation to those who are in Christ Jesus, who do not walk according to the flesh, but according to the Spirit.* —**Romans 8:1–2** NKJV

A Sincere Faith

According to Hebrews 11:1, "Faith is the substance of things hoped for, the evidence of things not seen." Elton Trueblood said, "Faith is not belief without proof, but trust without reservation." It is knowing that God cares, believing that God can, and trusting that God will.

In a broad sense, faith refers to a religious expression. While there are more religions than we can count, our faith as Christians rests upon God reconciling humanity unto Himself through the death, burial, and resurrection of Jesus Christ.

Faith can also refer to one's personal relationship with God as well as one's confidence in the power and providence of God. Faith is what turns belief into trust. Martin Luther said, "Miracles take place not because they are performed but because they are believed."

In recent generations, many believers struggle to shape their faith rather than allow their faith to shape them. The faith that we once embraced answered questions. The faith we now know questions answers.

The ancient Greco-Roman world loved marble sculptures. Over time, when sculptures got chipped or damaged, artists would fill in the blemishes with wax. To authenticate that a statue was undamaged, artists would stamp them with the words *sine* (which means "without") and *cera* (which means "wax"). That is where our word "sincere" comes from.

sine + *cere* = sincere

A sincere, authentic faith is dynamic not static. It is both powerful and productive. James 2:26 (NIV) says, "Faith without works is dead." While our faith saves us, it should serve others:

> *Suppose a brother or a sister is without clothes and daily food. If one of you says to them, "Go in peace; keep warm and well fed," but does nothing about their physical needs, what good is it?* —James 2:15–16 NIV

A sincere faith pleases God.

Without faith it is impossible to please God.
—Hebrews 11:6 NIV

During the Civil War, Abraham Lincoln met with a group of ministers for a prayer breakfast. One of the ministers said, "Mr. President, let us pray that God is on our side." President Lincoln responded, "No, gentlemen, let us pray that we are on God's side."

> *Search me, O God, and know my heart;*
> *test me and know my anxious thoughts.*
> *See if there is any offensive way in me,*
> *and lead me in the way everlasting.*
>
> **Psalm 139:23–24** niv

ACKNOWLEDGMENTS

We are indeed grateful for our editors: Reverend O. Christopher Buckner, Dr. Kimberly Ann Clark (Virginia Union University), Sherra Crawford, and Emma Shepard. Without this remarkable team, this project would not have been possible.

Much Love and Many Thanks!

BIBLIOGRAPHY

Angelou, Maya. *I Shall Not Be Moved*. New York, NY: Bantam, 1991.

Augustine. *The Confessions of St. Augustine*. New Kensington, PA: Whitaker House, 2019.

Bailey, E. K. *Farther In and Deeper Down*. Chicago, IL: Moody Publishers, 2005.

Baker, Ella. *Freedom Bound*. Hoboken, NJ: Wiley, 1999.

Baldwin, James. *The Fire Next Time*. New York, NY: Vintage, 1992.

Bonhoeffer, Dietrich. *The Cost of Discipleship*. Chicago, IL: Touchstone Books, 1995.

Bridges, Jerry. *The Pursuit of Holiness*. Colorado Springs, CO: NavPress Publishing Group, 2006.

Chambers, Oswald. *The Complete Works of Oswald Chambers*. Grand Rapids, MI: Our Daily Bread Publishing, 2013.

Evans, Tony. *The Promise: Experiencing God's Greatest Gift—the Holy Spirit*. Chicago, IL: Moody Publishers, 1996.

Jakes, T. D. *Intimacy with God: The Spiritual Worship of the Believer*. Bloomington, MN: Bethany House, 2003.

Jeremiah, David. *The Spiritual Warfare Answer Book*. Nashville, TN: Thomas Nelson, 2016.

Jones, R. Timothy. *Soul Care*. Shreveport, LA: Forward Press, 2020.

Keller, Timothy. *The Prodigal God*. New York, NY: Penguin Books, 2011.

Lewis, C. S. *Mere Christianity*. San Francisco, CA: HarperOne, 2015.

Menninger, Karl. *Whatever Became of Sin?* New York, NY: Hawthorn Books, 1973.

Nouwen, Henri J. M. *Here and Now: Living in the Spirit*. Spring Valley, NY: Crossroad Publishing, 1994.

Packer, J. I. *Keep In Step with the Spirit.* Grand Rapids, MI: Fleming H. Revell, 1986.

Sheen, Fulton. *Your Life is Worth Living.* Edinburgh, Scotland: Saint Andrew's Press, 2001.

Sproul, R. C. *The Mystery of the Holy Spirit.* Carol Stream, IL: Tyndale House Publishers, 1994.

Spurgeon, Charles H. *Morning and Evening.* Peabody, MA: Hendrickson Publishers, 1994.

Thurman, Howard. *Disciplines of the Spirit.* Richmond, IN: Friends United Press, 1963.

Tozer, A. W. *The Pursuit of God.* Camp Hills, PA: Wingspread Publishing, 1982.

Trueblood, Elton. *The Meditations of Elton Trueblood.* New York, NY: Harper and Row Publishers, 1975.

Tutu, Desmond. *An African Prayer Book.* Veghel, Netherlands: Image, 2006.

King, Martin Luther, Jr. *A Testament of Hope: The Essential Writings and Speeches.* San Francisco, CA: HarperOne, 2003.

ABOUT THE AUTHOR

R. Timothy Jones is married to the former Sherbrina M. Trammel and father of three fine children: Timothy Jr., Titus, and Mauri. He earned a Doctor of Ministry from Virginia Union University. Dr. Jones has served as pastor of the Peaceful Rest Missionary Baptist Church (The Family of Faith) since 1994.

In the summer 2008 issue, The *African American Pulpit* magazine cited him as one of "Twenty to Watch." He was also featured in the September 2019 issue of *Epitome* magazine. Dr. Jones has served as a denominational leader at the local, state, and national levels.

Dr. Jones is an Adjunct Professor of Religion at Jarvis Christian University. He is the author of *A Blessed and Highly Favored Life*, *Soul Care*, *Joy*, *Lessons Learned the Hard Way*, *Leave It on the Field*, and *The Spirit-filled Life*.

He is a 2015 Fellow of the Black Theology and Leadership Institute at Princeton Theological Seminary. Dr. Jones lives by three daily affirmations: "To thyself be true, to God be faithful, and to others be kind."

OTHER BOOKS BY R. TIMOTHY JONES

The Blessed and Highly Favored Life

Soul Care

Joy

Lessons Learned the Hard Way

Leave It on the Field

Made in the USA
Columbia, SC
12 June 2025